Dr. Kevin Leman

value-packed parenting

Workbook

SAMPSON
RESOURCES

4887 Alpha, Suite 220 • Dallas, Texas 75244 • (972) 387-2806 • (800) 371-5248 • FAX 972-387-0150

www.sampsonresources.com   info@sampsonresources.com

HOW TO USE THIS WORKBOOK

Your *Value-Packed Parenting* workbook is designed to accompany the 7-session video study by Dr. Kevin Leman. This workbook includes a new feature never before offered—a special narrative section at the beginning of each lesson that contains valuable content upon which the video lesson is based. This way, instead of leaving the session and trying to remember what Dr. Leman said in the video, you are able to take an expanded version of his video content home with you in the workbook. The workbook also includes a key scripture, discussion guide, application and prayer for each lesson. If at all possible, every participant should have his or her own workbook to use in the discussion/interaction time and to keep as a valuable parenting resource for years to come.

table of contents

Lesson 1

THE TEN BEST GIFTS YOU'LL EVER GIVE YOUR KIDS 4

It's Never Too Late to Become a Better Parent

Lesson 2

HOW TO LISTEN SO KIDS WILL TALK AND HOW TO TALK

SO KIDS WILL LISTEN 9

Staying Tuned In So They Don't Tune You Out

Lesson 3

DISCIPLINE ISN'T SPELLED P-U-N-I-S-H-M-E-N-T 15

Why Teaching and Learning Are Better than Punishment and Penalties

Lesson 4

TEN WAYS TO IMPROVE YOUR CHILD'S SELF-CONFIDENCE 20

A Step-by-Step Plan That Works Wonders

Lesson 5

CAUTION: ANGER AHEAD! 25

Observing the Warning Signs before Tempers Flare

Lesson 6

BIRTH ORDER—AND WHAT YOU NEED TO KNOW ABOUT IT 30

Recognizing Your Children's Differences and Turning Them into Advantages

Lesson 7

STANDING UP TO THE NEW GOLIATH 36

Helping Kids Overcome the Negative Influence of the Internet, the Media and Technology

The 10 Best Gifts You'll Ever Give Your Kids

It's Never Too Late to Become a Better Parent

Think with me for a minute, moms and dads.

How would it be, mom, to have your lanky 16 or 17-year-old son come home after school with two or three of his buddies, find you in the kitchen, come up behind you, lift you off the floor with a bear hug and say "How's it going, mom? You OK?" How would it be, dads, to have your 15 or 16-year-old daughter come in after school with two or three of her friends, throw her books down, come into the den where you are, jump in your lap and give you a big hug and kiss on the cheek—in front of her friends? You'd have to agree that it doesn't get any better than that.

The fact is, we've got one shot at raising our kids—a few years to get them ready for life on their own, because one day they're going to leave. They're going to pack up and move out! What I want to help you do is to get them ready. In a real sense, when we're raising our kids, we're packing their luggage so they'll be ready to leave home well-equipped with everything they'll need to live well-balanced, productive lives, independent of us. Are we going to fill their luggage with value… or filler? I suggest that we pack it full of value!

One of the most familiar verses in the Bible that relates to raising kids is one we're all familiar with—Proverbs 22:6 *"Train up a child in the way he should go: and when he is old, he will not depart from it."* (KJV) You know the word in that verse that is intriguing to me? It's the word "up." We're to train our kids "up." Not realizing it, many parents train their kids "down." Remember, our goal is to raise "rock-solid kids" who will one day be ready to leave home and live successfully on their own. I'm going to tell you later on how to train your kids "up" and not "down"!

Proverbs 22:6 in the New Living Translation reads, *"Teach your children to choose the right path, and when they are older, they will remain on it."* In the process of helping our children "choose the right path," we must discern differing paths for each child. It is natural to want to bring up all our children alike or train them the same way, but this verse implies that parents should discern the individuality and special strengths that God has given each child and train them "up" according to "the way *they* should go."

To do this, you need to take what I call the "long look." As a parent, you should look years down the road and develop a vision for how you'd like to see your kids turn out, then raise them to that vision. Begin to treat your kids as though they're in the process of becoming what you envision them to be. If you have no plan or vision of where you're headed with your kids, then "any road will take you there." What does a good kid "look" like anyway? What do you want your son or daughter to "look" like when they leave home? If you make a list of the truly important things you need to do to raise rock-solid, well-balanced kids, you won't have a long list—you'll have a short list. After all, your goal is not to be a perfect parent—just a good and responsible parent. You can make some mistakes—you can miss on some things—but there are a few things you just can't afford to miss on.

Based on a career in education as a Assistant Dean of Students at the University of Arizona, a private practice as a clinical psychologist, personal experience as a parent, and having written 30 or so books on parenting and family issues, I want to share with you what I call the "BIG TEN"—the 10 best, most valuable gifts you'll ever give your kids. Again, you can miss on some things, but you don't want to miss on these ten! You and I both know that we have a window of time when it's easier to mold and train our kids, but regardless of where you are in the process of raising your kids, it's never too late to become a better parent.

Deuteronomy 11:19 says, *"Teach them to your children. Talk about them when you are at home and when you are away on a journey, when you are lying down and when you are getting up again."* Teach "what" to your children? Verse 18 says *"teach these words of mine."* In other words, teach your children God's ways and principles. I promise you, everything I'm going to share with you in this study fits within God's ways. These 10 best gifts you'll ever give your kids fit within God's ways. Here they are.

1. Give them safety and security. Your kids have to know that they can trust you to take care of them and keep them safe. Do you know what is the most critical year for developing this trust? Between birth to age 1! Kids need to feel secure, live in an open environment where they can move freely and safely through the various stages of development. Again, a child's first taste of trust is in the first year of life. Developmental psychologist Eric Erickson calls this first stage of life *Trust vs. Mistrust.*

2. Give them love. I know it sounds like an obvious truth, but it is profoundly critical that children experience your affection, acceptance, a sense of belonging, love for your spouse, and love for Christ. If you have no spouse, then your kids must see love for close relatives, friends, Christ. It is imperative that children see deep, committed love modeled in the home.

> It is imperative that children see deep, committed love modeled in the home.

3. Give them attention. Spend time with them—quantity time, not just quality time. *Talk* to them; engage them in conversation, collaboration, sharing ideas, thoughts, plans. *Play* with them—when they're little, roll around on the floor with them, do crafts with them, read to them. When they're in elementary school, play outside with them, go to their games, recitals, parent's night at school; play video games with them. When they're in junior high and high school, knock yourself out to watch them do what they do, and be sure they know that you get a bang out of it! Then *help* them. Several hundred high school kids that were surveyed said they desperately needed their parents' help in lots of ways, but just weren't comfortable going to them for help—and their parents didn't offer it! They had to get help somewhere else or do without.

4. Give them space. Kids need room to grow and develop into who God uniquely designed them to be. Kids don't want to be crowded, especially when they get into the pre-adolescent and adolescent years. They need the freedom to succeed and freedom to fail. Both are important.

5. Give them an example. Live out the values and virtues you want your children to embrace—consistently; walk your talk; don't teach one thing, then do just the opposite. Live in the reality that "you are being watched." Do you realize that this is one of the best ways kids learn? By watching. You don't have to *teach* kids everything— some things they learn automatically by watching you.

6. Give them direction. Psalm 32:8 says, *The Lord says, 'I will guide you along the best pathway for your life. I will advise you and watch over you.'* In other words, God gives direction to us as we give direction to our children. What do you teach them? Values, virtues, what's acceptable and what's not; right from wrong. You don't have to teach a child to be bad; he comes into the world bent on that. You have to teach him to be good. Ask yourself: What are the specific values you are imparting to your kids? Is it happening by accident or is it planned and monitored? What are some of the values you think are important anyway? How do you teach values best? By example, that's how. By recognizing them in your kids and expressing appreciation for them.

> You don't have to *teach* kids everything— some things they learn automatically by watching you.

7. Give them boundaries. Boundaries and rules are not negative. They are positive. Rules, baselines and boundaries *make* the game. Without them you can't even play the game—any game! Boundaries not only pertain to the kids in the family or the players *on* the field, they pertain to those *off* the field. They protect your kids from undesirable outside influences that are ready to creep into their lives. A good boundary keeps things *in* and at the same time keeps things *out*.

8. Give them responsibility. Kids must learn to contribute and give back to the home and to other members of the family, e.g., helping with chores, jobs, etc. Give your kids an understanding of what it means to be accountable, dependable, and responsible for their own words and actions. Teaching children to accept and carry out responsibility is a key factor in building healthy self-esteem. If you don't assign your kids responsibilities, they may get the idea that you don't think they could handle them anyway.

9. Give them discipline. Proverbs 3:11-12 says *My child, don't ignore it when the Lord disciplines you, and don't be discouraged when he corrects you. For the Lord corrects those he loves, just as a father corrects a child in whom he delights.* Why do we want to pack our kids' bags with discipline? Because we love them! We delight in them! Discipline consists of teaching and learning, and if you major on that, you can minimize punishment and penalties. Teaching and learning encourage everyone, while punishment and penalties hurt everyone.

10. Give them biblical instruction. How? Through personal faith in Jesus Christ and spiritual growth in a Bible-based church. The primary place for kids to develop spiritually is the home. The next is church. Who or what is the key to your child's spiritual growth? The parents are. So, are *you* growing spiritually? You've heard it said that "a stream can't rise any higher than its source." As you grow deeper in your faith, you'll be able to help your children develop in their faith. And faith in God provides the foundation upon which their life experiences come to rest. In fact, their faith becomes the pallet of colors they use to paint their own unique picture on the canvas we call life.

Now you might expand on this list of "The 10 Best Gifts You'll Ever Give Your Kids" or develop your own list from scratch, but I believe whatever you come up with will probably fit into these ten. Again, you can miss on some things, but don't miss on these if you want your parenting to be "value-packed." If you want your kids to WIN, give them these 10! And start today! Remember… it's never too late to become a better parent.

discussion

1. Think back for a moment to when your first child was born and how you felt about your new parenting responsibility. Were you worried, fearful, concerned or confident in your ability to parent effectively? Try to recall your thoughts and jot them down below. Share as a group.

   _____

   _____

2. If you ask your friends where they learned how to parent, what would they say? What specific steps have you taken that have helped you become a better parent? (books, seminars, classes, etc.)

   _____

   _____

3. Write down the names of a few specific individuals who have had a positive influence on you as you observed how they raised their kids.

   _____

   _____

   Now jot down some specific qualities and characteristics that these parents had in common that set them apart, then share with the group.

   _____

   _____

4. In the video lesson we talked about the importance of parents taking the "long look" and having a vision of what they want their kids to "look" like when they're ready to leave home. Do you have a mental picture of how you want your kids to look in terms of character traits, values, and spiritual development? If so, write a brief description in the space below.

   _____

   _____

5. The scripture theme of this lesson is a very familiar one. In the KJV, Proverbs 22:6 says, *"Train up a child in the way he should go: and when he is old, he will not depart from it."* What do you feel is significant about these key words and phrases?

   train - _____

   up - _____

   child - _____

   in the way he (she) should go - _____

6. Dr. Jane Nelson, an educational psychologist, suggest three "Rs" that are easy to remember, but profoundly important when raising kids. Jot them down and beside each one write a brief thought as to how you can help your child develop in that particular "R."

R_____ — _____

R_____ — _____

R_____ — _____

application

lifescene

Ruthie and her cousin Olivia, ages 6 and 5, are enjoying a summer afternoon at Ruthie's house when out of the blue they decide they want to set up a lemonade stand in the front yard near the street. They excitedly pitch the idea to Ashley, Ruthie's mom, who immediately sees possibilities for some combined fun and learning. She leads the kids to develop their own simple list of what they will need and how they are going to arrange their stand, careful not to tell them step-by-step exactly what to do. She helps the kids decide on the ingredients for the lemonade, and how to gather the pitchers, cups, napkins, ice, table, chairs and signs. They also have to decide how much to charge, how to greet and treat their customers, and what they will do with whatever money they make. They immediately go to work to get everything set up. After multiple trips back and forth to the house carrying out their supplies, they are open for business.

If you were driving down the street and saw Ruthie and Olivia's lemonade stand, would you stop and buy some lemonade? Why or why not? Do you see any of the three "Rs" at work here? Make a few notes and discuss with the group.

_____

_____

_____

_____

prayer

Dear Father, with all my heart I want to be the parent my children need me to be. From this time forward I'm going to develop a vision for what they can become one day when it's time for them to leave home, then I want to pack into their lives those qualities and attributes that will get them there. It's a relief to realize that I don't have to be a perfect parent to my children. But starting today, I'm going to try to become a better parent. My kids deserve it, and with your help, I'm going to do it. In Jesus' name, Amen.

— It's never too late to become a better parent. —

How to Listen So Kids Will Talk & How to Talk So Kids Will Listen

Staying Tuned In So They Don't Tune You Out

Listening and talking. It's something we do every day and think nothing of it.

Yet between parents and children, there is probably no other activity that is as profoundly important to the health of the relationship. Listening and talking represent communication, and communication is the track that relationships run on.

What does listening, talking, conversing, exchanging ideas, collaborating with another person say about two people anyway? It says that they are interested in each other, value each other's thoughts and feelings, are willing to expose their inner concerns and vulnerabilities, are reaching out for help, counsel or advice, and willing to offer the same in return. It's a fact of life that people we are comfortable around, we listen to and talk to. People we are not comfortable around, we tend not to listen to and talk to.

Believe me, kids know if you are really listening to them and are interested in what they have to say. And if they figure out that you're not listening to them and don't have much to say to them—other than directing and correcting— they'll begin to believe that they're not really very important to you. You can say otherwise, but in their heart they'll know better.

So parents, if you want to stay tuned in so your kids don't tune you out, here's what I suggest you do.

Talk to your kids—a lot! About anything and everything! Let this be the silent, but understood agreement between you and your kids: that you will listen as long as they want to talk! But don't make the mistake of thinking that they want your advice and counsel at *all* times. Sometimes they don't—they just want a listening ear. They are aware that you know a lot, but they don't want to know everything you know. It isn't necessary to come back with corrective phrases, trying to improve on your kids' perspective, evaluating, judging, and ultimately proving that you know more than they know. This puts them off, makes them feel inadequate and uncomfortable. Try responding with "I never thought about it

key scripture

Let everything you say be good and helpful, so that your words will be an encouragement to those who hear them.

Ephesians 4:29

that way," or "that's an interesting way to look at it," or "I can tell you've given this a lot of thought." When you have the chance to engage your child in conversation, be smart about it and leave the child feeling good about himself and the exchange.

Learn the difference between responding and reacting. If you go back to a doctor for an evaluation after a previous visit, and he says, "Ah, you've responded to the medicine," is that good or bad? It's good. If he says, "Ah, you've reacted to the medicine," is that good or bad? Bad. I'm not saying that reacting is never the right thing to do. Certainly there are times when we need to react, but all too often, parents tend to react in a knee-jerk kind of way that alarms their kids needlessly and makes them feel belittled. If a kid knocks over his milk at the breakfast table, you can *react* and get all bent out of shape over it, saying, "What a mess you've made! Now get down and clean it up! No more milk for you!" On the other hand, you can *respond* and say, "Uh-oh. There's a towel by the sink you can use to clean that up. Accidents like that can happen when your glass is too close to the edge of the table." All I'm suggesting is that if you want to keep the lines of communication open, practice *responding* instead of *reacting*. The truth is, responding and reacting reflect your personal attitudes. Move with caution so you can keep your relationship with your kids positive and open.

Keep the lines of communication open; practice *responding* instead of *reacting*.

Here is a sample of the kind of responses and reactions I'm talking about. Read them through, then ask yourself, "If I were the child approaching my mom or dad with a proposal or idea, how would I want them to talk to me?"

POSITIVE RESPONSES
That Reflect a Positive Attitude

- I'm open to that.
- That's an interesting idea.
- This has possibilities. Keep talking.
- You're doing some good thinking.
- I think you may be onto something.
- I'm sure willing to listen.
- All I want is what's good for you.
- I know you're bound to have some good reasons for doing what you did.
- I can see some possibilities in your idea.
- I'd like to understand your position more completely.
- It's definitely worth talking over with the family.
- Sounds like you've given this a lot of careful thought.
- Why didn't I think of that?
- We can't say *yes* or *no* right now, but we'll definitely consider it.
- Let's look at it from some other perspectives, then make our decision.
- Help me understand the situation a little better.
- Whatever you decide, I'm on your side.
- We may not be able to do it just now, but it deserves a good hard look.
- Your idea sounds good. Tell me more.
- Why don't you go ahead and make the decision, then tell me what you've decided. I'll be interested to know your thoughts.
- I can see why you've asked.
- It may not be possible right now, but it's something we'll want to consider.
- Let's look at some more options.
- Let's be sure this is the absolute best thing for you and everyone concerned.
- After we think it through together, I think you'll understand why it's not best.
- Let's leave personalities out of it and just focus on the problem.
- I'm sure you've got some good reasons for thinking this way.
- Your reasoning makes a lot of sense to me.
- Whoa! Look at this! I knew you'd do it right!
- I can't think of a better way, so let's do it your way.

NEGATIVE REACTIONS
That Reflect a Negative Attitude

- Be quiet and listen to me for a change!
- N-O! No! No!! NO!!!
- I gave you my answer, so that's THAT!
- It won't work, so forget it!
- I can't believe you even asked me that!
- Sometimes your thinking scares me!
- That sounds about like something you'd say!
- You think maybe if I drew you a picture, you'd catch on?
- You never let up, do you?
- You know what I think, so don't even ask!
- A question like that doesn't even deserve an answer!

- You ought to know better than that!
- You're not paid to think!
- First of all, the decision is not yours to make!
- I told your mother this would happen! And bingo! It's happened!
- Who do you think you are anyway?
- The trouble with you is, you never listen!
- I told you so, didn't I?
- Chill out! We can handle this very well without you!
- I don't want to hear any more of your thoughts on the subject!
- Nobody asked for your opinion!
- What makes you think I should listen to you anyway!
- I've already told you once! Now drop it!
- You'll only mess it up again. We'll handle it this time!
- You NEVER learn, do you?
- There! SEE? You've done it again!
- I knew from the start I shouldn't have trusted you!
- I'm not going to forget this for a long time!
- Let me do it. You'll just mess it up!
- If a bird had your brain, he'd fly sideways!

Realize that your tone of voice is a reflection of your attitude. Colossians 4:6 says, *Let your conversation be gracious and effective…* Why? The scripture goes on to say *…so that you will have the right answer for everyone.* Not just the right answer in terms of *what* you say, but *how* you say it. Are you familiar with the "93-7 Principle" in communication? Basically, it says that only 7% of the effectiveness of communication comes directly from the words we use, while 93% comes from *how* we say what we say…how we use those words. If your tone of voice is calm and relaxed, your communication will be much more "gracious and effective."

Let your communication be non-threatening rather than threatening. After all, what kid wants to be threatened all the time? You say, "But she won't mind me any other way!" Yes, she will. Kids who have to be threatened all the time have learned that threats are often a reflection of their parents' feelings of inner frustration, uncertainty and insecurity. What kids really need to see is parents who understand their authority and position, and who can speak firmly and courteously when directing or correcting them. If you as a parent understand your position and

authority, you won't feel that you have to scream and yell commands. Just calmly say, "I guess since you're not feeding the dog regularly like you're supposed to, he is going to begin losing weight and become sickly. How sad that is. He deserves better." Monitor these and similar situations, then simply follow through as necessary—with firmness and certainty.

Speak more in statements than questions.
Questions often suggest a hierarchy: that the person asking the questions is "up here" and the person being asked the questions is "down there." Instead of hitting your son with "How did you do on that test today?"…use the statement, "I'll bet that test today was tough." Then maybe use a question that focuses on the test instead of the child, something like, "Was the test as hard as you thought it was going to be?" "I'll bet all your studying paid off, huh?" In other words, when you do have to ask questions—and all parents do—ask them in as non-threatening a manner as possible. Somehow kids seem to learn over time that adults use questions to draw them out so they can attack their position. The goal is to draw them out so you can listen to them and hear them out. Whatever you do, keep them talking!

> Your countenance and attitude can either encourage or discourage conversation.

Once again, let me make a suggestion that will pay rich dividends over the years: *Be willing to listen to your kids talk to you anytime and anywhere, for as long as they want to talk.* I repeat, keep them talking to you. Stop listening to them, and they'll find someone else to talk to.

Have a "yes" face. Get yourself a facelift! It won't cost you anything, and you can perform it on yourself! Your countenance and attitude can either encourage or discourage conversation, collaboration, and exchange of thoughts. What a shame for a child to always see a "no" face. He knows what the answer is before he asks. "No! I've already told you that! So don't ask again, or I'll…!" Parents who lack inner security and confidence or simply don't know any better talk to down to their kids. Sure, there's a time to be firm and declarative. But if you're determined to say "no" or react strongly time after time, be prepared for your relationship with your kids to suffer.

There's nothing wrong with "no." In fact, there are times when "no" is just as positive as "yes." But too many "no's" said with a cold, harsh tone and very little explanation tell the child that he's got to get what he wants another way, a way that may very well be inappropriate and unacceptable.

Collaborate: exchange ideas and observations. Collaborating and exchanging ideas are perfect ways to create opportunities to listen. Look for ways to draw your kids into a conversation with non-threatening questions or statements pertaining to something the kids are interested in. On purpose—ask your daughter for her opinion as to which tie looks best. Then say, "That's interesting. Why do you think so?" And don't look her in the eye. After she answers, say, "You know, I think you're right about that. Thanks. I may need some more advice later on." In other words, look for ways to engage your child in a thinking process that will give you a reason to affirm him or her and encourage more of the same. "Which of these wallpapers do you think looks best with the furniture?" "Which shade of trim paint do you like best with the wall color?" "Where in the flowerbed should I plant this rose bush?" or "Who do you pick to win the game?" or "What do you think is the best way to load this in the trunk?"

It's OK to ask "why." Just do it in a non-threatening way. The more practice a child has expressing reasons for thinking and formulating an opinion—without being put down or made to feel

> If you are not the primary source of encouragement to your kids, who is going to encourage them?

inadequate—the more he or she will continue to think, reason and make decisions, and the better chance you will have for an positive relationship based on open, free lines of communication. Collaborate means "to work or labor with."

Always project an "I'm open to you" attitude to your kids. Make it a motto you live by. Why "I'm open to you"? Because it says, "Come at me with your ideas, thoughts and propositions…anything. You're worth listening to, and that's what I'm here for. Whatever your needs are, I'm your best source for meeting them. So come to me first. I won't put you down or make you feel stupid or inadequate." Plus, an "I'm open to you" attitude is encouraging to the child. The Apostle Paul says in 1 Thessalonians 5:11, *So encourage each other and build each other up, just as you are already doing.* Paul is talking to the Christians who live in the city of Thessalonica who are soon going to be facing very difficult times. He's also talking to us! If you are not the primary source of encouragement to your kids, who is going to encourage them?

When your kids come to you, they need to be thinking, "I can talk to my mom and dad about anything, and I won't be embarrassed, judged, evaluated, or made to feel stupid, selfish, or inadequate. That's pretty cool." Kids may not think with these exact words, but that's what they will be feeling.

So parents, when your kids come at you with a proposal, remain calm regardless of how far-fetched the proposal might be. Use some of the sample "positive responses" instead of the "negative reactions," and you'll see that listening and talking can foster the satisfying relationship you've always wanted. Stay tuned in to *them* so they don't tune *you* out.

discussion

1. Think about the title of this session for a moment: HOW TO LISTEN SO KIDS WILL TALK AND HOW TO TALK SO KIDS WILL LISTEN. Make a few notes and discuss with the group any significance you see in this title and why it emphasizes listening before talking.

_____

_____

2. From the time your kids were born until the time they began to talk, it was necessary for you to do a lot of listening. Why was that? What could you possibly learn by listening to a child who has not yet learned to talk?

_____

_____

3. When children learn to talk and gradually get better at it, one thing is certain: they'll wear you out talking to you and asking questions, often saying the same thing over and over. Why do you think they do this? What unmet needs are they expressing?

_____

_____

4. Some parents become frustrated—they've "had enough"—and often react

when, in fact, a better choice would be to respond _____

_____

5. Look over the list of _positive responses_ and _negative reactions_ and see if you can add any colorful ones of your own! Discuss with the group.

_____

_____

_____

_____

6. Jot down three or four reasons why you should listen to your kids, regardless of their age.

    a. _____

    b. _____

    c. _____

    d. _____

7. Some kids talk freely and openly with their parents right on through the adolescent years. Why do you think this is? Make some notes and discuss together.

_____

_____

8. Many kids approach the adolescent years and begin to withdraw and avoid talking to their parents—even become secretive. Why do you think this is? If they are not talking to their parents, who are they talking to and why? Make some notes and discuss as a group some specific factors and personal experiences.

_____

_____

application

lifescene

It seems to Kathy, who desperately wants to have a child, that her next-door neighbor Sara must have the ideal family. One Saturday, she sees Sara planting some flowers, so she walks over to chat and see what she's planting. After a few minutes admiring her new flowerbed, her curiosity gets the best of her, and she says, "Sara, I've observed your kids for five years now. I know they're bound not to be perfect, but they sure seem to be! They look like they've got it together. They're lively, have lots of friends, behave themselves, really respect you and Bud, and seem to like going to church. They get along great with everybody. Plus, I understand they do well in school. I'm curious. What's your secret?"

In a few words, jot down what you think Sara told Kathy, then discuss with the group. Do you think they practiced Ephesians 4:29 in their home?

_____

_____

_____

_____

prayer

Dear Lord, I want my children to be open to me and comfortable with my teaching and counsel during these critical years. Please help me to hear them with my whole heart. I want to listen to their thoughts and ideas attentively and respond respectfully so they will keep talking to me. In Jesus' name, Amen.

— It's never too late to become a better parent. —

Discipline Isn't Spelled P-U-N-I-S-H-M-E-N-T

Why Teaching and Learning Are Better than Punishment and Penalties

I believe one of the greatest responsibilities God gives parents is to nurture and guide their children—as Proverbs 13:24 says, *to discipline them*. While it is not always easy to discipline children, one thing we can be sure of is that lack of discipline puts parents' love in question because it shows a lack of concern for the character development of their children. What Proverbs 13:24 is telling us is that we should not be *afraid* to discipline our kids. It is an act of love.

Two words parents are fairly familiar with these days are "discipline" and "punishment." We'd all agree that kids are going to misbehave, and when they do, parents need to respond. Unfortunately, too many times they *react* with punishment and penalties when they could *respond* with appropriate on-the-job teaching and correction that would be of lasting benefit to the child. That's what discipline is all about—*learning*. In fact, the biblical word "disciple" means "learner" or "one who learns."

There's a school of thought that says "Get people to do what you want them to do through fear of reprisal or punishment." Another approach says "Get people to do what you want them to do by loving them, teaching them, treating them with respect, helping them grow and develop, and rewarding them." Does the second approach always work with children in every situation? No. Misbehavior must be dealt with, and sometimes it must be dealt with by applying negative consequences that make things uncomfortable for the one who is misbehaving. I just happen to believe, however, that the second approach is the better of the two.

Here are a few suggestions concerning discipline—teaching and learning.

Consider discipline a privilege, not a chore. Consider discipline something you *get* to do, not just something you *have* to do. What could be better than having the opportunity to give your kids direction, teach them a valuable lesson that can help them avoid some long-range disaster, or that will contribute to their character develop-

ment? Stop looking at discipline with the negative "Oh, no!" connotation, and start seeing it as a positive "Oh, yes!" opportunity where your kids can learn something. Discipline doesn't mean spanking, time out, sitting in the corner, or losing all privileges! Take this matter of discipline seriously and do what you do with a purpose in mind. Don't try to catch your kids doing something wrong. That won't be hard to do. Try to catch them doing something right. Then recognize it and express appreciation for it, maybe with a description of how it makes you and others feel.

> Consider discipline something you *get* to do, not just something you *have* to do.

Keep the highest form of discipline your goal: self-discipline. Your ultimate goal should be to teach your kids to discipline themselves. As soon as possible, encourage them to set their alarm clocks, get up on time, dress themselves, be at the table on time, be ready to head out for school on time, feed the fish, do their homework promptly, etc. In other words, start as early as possible allowing kids to do things for themselves just like you've taught them. This doesn't mean you don't do things for them…or that you make them do everything for themselves. Just don't sidetrack them on the road to independence by doing everything for them. That's not *enabling* your kids—that's *disabling* them!

An excellent way to teach self-discipline is to write a list of things that are important for a young child to do, e.g., chores, small responsibilities, etc., and post the list on the side of the fridge as visible reminders. When the kids meet the requirements that are listed, apply stickers or stars to indicate completion. Don't, however, make the mistake of bragging on what a good kid he is for doing his chores. Doing his chores doesn't make him a good kid! You don't want him to fall into the trap of feeling that he's got to get his daily self-esteem boost based on how he performs his chores on a daily basis. Instead, show appreciation for what he's done and describe how it makes you and others feel, as well as how he should feel.

Think for a moment. Why on earth would kids ever want to be self-disciplined, organized and able to do things for themselves? *First,* because they've seen you set the example. *Second,* they feel your recognition and appreciation of how this contributes to the well-being of the entire family. *Third,* they hear and observe among their peers the conflict and confusion that's going on in their families because of lack of discipline. *Fourth,* they experience the rewards and effects of doing things the way they've been taught…courtesy, manners, helping with chores, a positive attitude, and so on.

Use discipline to "enable." A common trap that parents fall into is doing too much for their kids. They think they don't have time to let kids do things for themselves…the kids won't do it exactly right…the parent needs the gratification of "mothering"…parents themselves are disorganized…mistakenly thinking it's their job to "do" for their kids. Again, doing too much and giving too much to kids does not *enable* them— it *disables* them. Parents who have a hard time letting go must realize that letting go is a process that should begin by degrees early in a child's life. As soon as he can feed himself, you don't feed him anymore. As soon as he can use the potty by himself, you no longer assist him. When she can decide what to wear and dress herself, let her do it; as soon as she's passed driver's ed and received her permanent license, you don't have to ride with her and police her anymore. When kids can show that they know when to come home at night, you don't have to lay down the law to them. This is what discipline is all about. Do more disciplining and you'll have to do less punishing. Punishment and penalties always take a back seat to steady, consistent discipline.

Use discipline for correction. Proverbs 6:23 says, *These commands and this teaching are a lamp to light the way ahead of you. The correction of discipline is the way to life.*

Correction need not be intimidating and hurtful. It just comes with the territory of teaching and learning. Does correction sometimes have the connotation of negative consequences? Yes. But the difference in discipline with negative consequences and punishment with penalties and negative consequences is *how you apply it*. With discipline, you emphasize the positive lessons to be learned along with corrective measures to help the child learn, without attacking or belittling him. With punishment and penalties, too often the emphasis is on the child himself, or he's lumped together with the bad things he has done and then left to wallow in his misery. And unfortunately, everyone in the family usually has to participate in the misery. Punishment hurts everybody. Hebrews 12:11 says, *No discipline is enjoyable while it is happening—it is painful! But afterward there will be a quiet harvest of right living for those who are trained in this way.*

Is punishment a necessary part of life? Yes. Negative consequences of unacceptable behavior are absolutely necessary, and they can take a variety of forms. The lesson here, however, is to focus on discipline—teaching and learning—so you can minimize punishment and penalties. Remember, the biblical word "disciple" means "learner" or "one who learns."

What would be the result of forgetting about "discipline" and focusing on "punishment"? A family full of unhappy campers, that's what! When you're developing a football team, a debate team, a soccer team, a choir, whatever…what do you emphasize? Discipline or punishment? Discipline! Sure, the penalties for being off-sides or grabbing a facemask are out there; an unexcused absence from practice may mean running laps. But still, your goal is to learn to practice and play by the rules. The purpose of being sidelined or penalized is to get your attention with a negative consequence so you'll be more respectful of the game and the other players, and get to enjoy playing the game.

If you're trying to grow a family where the kids behave themselves and get along with everyone in the family, you don't jump down their throats every time they mess up. You say, "Hey, this is not how we treat members of our family, and we've talked about it several times. I think this calls for a negative consequence (you've taught them what a negative consequence is). What do you think it should be so you'll learn to treat your sister with respect?" Let him think it through and make a suggestion. If you need to alter it, alter it. Then enforce it.

> With discipline, you emphasize the positive lessons to be learned…

Want peace of mind in your home? Proverbs 29:17 tells you how. It says, *Discipline your children, and they will give you happiness and peace of mind.* So how do you spell "discipline." D-i-s-c-i-p-l-i-n-e. Not p-u-n-i-s-h-m-e-n-t.

Discipline works!

discussion

1. Have you ever been in a restaurant and a couple sitting next to you allowed their kids to run around between the tables, playing chase and making all kinds of racket while you were trying to enjoy a quiet dinner? If so, how would you finish these statements?

■ If those were my kids, I'd _____ !

■ Some parents just don't have a _____ !

■ If I owned this restaurant, I'd_____ !

■ If those kids act like that in front of their parents, think _____ !

2. Why do you think some parents are so permissive when it comes to their children's behavior?

_____

_____

3. Can some parents simply tolerate more than others? Are they lazy? Do they not love their kids? Are they afraid they will stunt their children's creative development if they're not allowed to set the restaurant on fire? Make some notes and discuss with the group.

_____

_____

4. Complete this verse—Proverbs 13:24: _If you _____ to discipline your children, it proves you _____ love them; if you love your children, you will be _____ to discipline them._

5. "Discipline" and "punishment" are two words we hear often. In your own way of thinking, how would you say discipline differs from punishment? Make some notes and share as a group how you distinguish between these two words.

_____

_____

6. Jot down some specific things you do to discipline—teach, instruct, correct—your kids in a positive manner so you don't have to punish them.

_____

_____

7. Quickly list some areas where you feel that your children are lacking in discipline and need to show improvement.

_____

_____

_____

8. If your ultimate goal is for your kids to develop self-discipline, what specific steps can you take to help them become more self-disciplined?

_____

_____

application

lifescene

Courtney, a 16-year old high school sophomore, is going out with friends on a Friday night. When her friends came to the door to pick her up, her dad grilled her as to where they are going, a play-by-play run-down as to what they'd be doing, who and how many would be in the car, etc. Then he told her to be home by 11:00 p.m. and not a minute later. As she was leaving, he caught her attention and gave her a little threatening wink that seemed to say, "Have a good time, but if you're late, you'll be sorry." Well, Courtney and her friends had a good time, but she arrived home at 11:05 p.m., five minutes late. Her dad met her at the door, told her she'd been irresponsible and that she'd be grounded for two weeks. The mother was standing within earshot listening.

What do you think the mother was thinking? If you'd been the father (or mother in charge), how would you have handled the situation from start to finish? Is there such a thing as over-reacting with punishment when you could have treated a situation in a completely different manner and scored a victory on all fronts? How could the situation have been handled so that everyone involved could have "won"—Courtney, her friends, the parents, etc.?

_____

_____

_____

_____

prayer

Dear Father, help me to understand that for our kids to learn the important lessons of life, someone must teach them—and I am that someone. Instead of raining down punishment to prove a point or to prove my authority, I want to teach valuable lessons within an environment of grace and forgiveness. Just help to keep my eyes open. In Jesus' name, Amen.

— It's never too late to become a better parent. —

Ten Ways to Improve Your Child's Self-Confidence

A Step-by-Step Plan That Works Wonders

key scripture

The Lord gave me a message. He said, 'I knew you before I formed you in your mother's womb. Before you were born I set you apart and appointed you as my spokesman to the world. O Sovereign Lord,' I said, 'I can't speak for you! I'm too young!' 'Don't say that,' the Lord replied, 'for you must go wherever I send you and say whatever I tell you. And don't be afraid of the people, for I will be with you and take care of you. I, the Lord, have spoken!'

Jeremiah 1:4-7

The prophet Jeremiah was "appointed" by God as "spokesman to the world." Now if God were speaking specifically to parents today in Jeremiah 1:4-7, he might have said, *'I knew you before I formed you in your mother's womb. Before you were born I set you apart and appointed you to be my spokesman to these little kids. O Sovereign Lord, I've decided I'm too young and inexperienced!' 'Don't say that,' the Lord says, 'for you must go wherever I send you and say whatever I tell you. And don't be afraid of these little people, for I will be with you and take care of you. I won't let them drive you nuts and make you jump off a building! I, the Lord, have spoken!'*

I think we all realize that it takes work to be good parents, and one of the things good parents are most concerned about is that their kids develop strong self-confidence. I want to give you a 10-point step-by-step plan that works wonders!

Want to see your kids grow in self-confidence?
1. Bless them. Make sure they know that they have your blessing. It has been said that "the eyes and ears of parents become mirrors into which children look in order to define themselves in terms of their self-confidence and self-worth." In other words, your kids need to be able to look at you and hear you say through your attitudes and words that you approve of them and believe in them. There are few people in the world you would die for, but you'd die for your kids. Your children need your blessing, and when they look into your eyes, they should recognize a blessing that says, "You've got exciting possibilities and potential, and I can't wait to see what you're going to accomplish with your life. You may have some ups and downs along the way, but you can always know that I believe in you." Or that blessing might suggest something like this: "I don't know about other kids, but I know about you. You've got what it takes to do something significant in life! I'll always be in your corner." Blessing your children gives them confidence in much the same way that a football player feels when the coach gives him some instruction on the sidelines, slaps him on the back and pushes him out on the field screaming, "You can do it!"

Want to see your kids' self-confidence improve?
2. Teach them to contribute. To whom? To the family and to others. You do this by assigning

them responsibilities that are appropriate for where they are in life. When they do contribute, remind them of what they are doing. They need to hear that they are contributing and helping with chores and responsibilities. Observe what your kids do best and encourage them in those areas. Look for opportunities to involve them in areas where they can excel. Children like to help, but are often shooed away with the impression that they are not really needed or wanted, and couldn't help out anyway. Look for ways that your kids can contribute, then acknowledge what they've done. They'll love it. If they want to help you paint, let them. You can always come back and touch it up. If they want to help you replace the septic tank, let them!

Want to improve your children's self-confidence? **3. Teach them to think, reason, and make decisions.** Just monitor the process so they don't put themselves in harm's way. Every outcome of a decision doesn't have to be perfect or completely in line with what you as the parent might decide. But so what? It's OK. Instead of answering all their questions with a quick, automatic answer, answer their question with a non-threatening question, almost as though you are asking the question of yourself as well. The idea is to get them to think *with* you, in step *with* you, so that one day they'll be able to think on their own, *apart* from you. That way, the questions won't put them on the spot and make them feel like they're taking some kind of test.

And when you do answer a child's question, don't go into some long discourse and tell him everything you know on the subject. What a turn-off to kids! Eventually, they're liable to stop asking you anything. The old line is, "Don't tell them more than they want to know." Sometimes they don't really even want an answer; they just want you to know what's on their mind or what they're dealing with at the moment.

Get their opinions and thoughts, and lead them through a logical reasoning process. The more good decisions a child can make on his own, the better he feels about himself, and the more in touch he is with his own abilities and potential. Small decisions are the building blocks upon which the confidence to make bigger decisions is based.

Want to build your kids' self-confidence? **4. Be available to them.** When you send a soldier up to the front lines, he'll go with much more confidence if you've equipped him well and if he knows that you're back there providing information and support. If he thinks you've simply dropped him off and hightailed it, he'll blink and shrink! Likewise, a kid needs to know his parents are available to him…to help him, hear him out, listen to his perspective, give him a couple of options he hasn't thought of, help him figure out what to do. Talk to him attentively, not over a book, newspaper or TV. Just don't stare him in the eye all the time. Be available to him. There's nothing wrong with saying to him at a random moment (without looking him in the eye), "Son, I guess everything's going OK. You know I'm available if anything ever comes up that you need to bounce off me. I'd be more than glad to think anything through with you." And leave it at that. Just don't overdo it. It turns kids off.

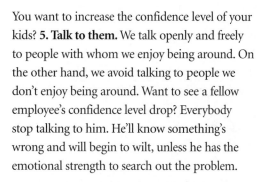

Parents need to learn that glaring at kids directly in the eye is like holding a double-barreled shotgun in their face. They feel put on the spot, intimidated and under a microscope. Try talking to them as though you are letting them read your thoughts, without looking them directly in the eye. They feel more openness and freedom as opposed to feeling hemmed in and scrutinized. On the other hand, when they really want your attention, give them natural and attentive—but not glaring—eye contact.

> Glaring at kids directly in the eye is like holding a double-barreled shotgun in their face.

You want to increase the confidence level of your kids? **5. Talk to them.** We talk openly and freely to people with whom we enjoy being around. On the other hand, we avoid talking to people we don't enjoy being around. Want to see a fellow employee's confidence level drop? Everybody stop talking to him. He'll know something's wrong and will begin to wilt, unless he has the emotional strength to search out the problem.

Teach your kids that they can talk to you about anything, that their thoughts are valuable and worth hearing. They can propose anything, ask for anything, get advice about anything…and in so doing that they will not be put down, compared, judged, embarrassed, or made to feel dumb and stupid. Let them know that they may need more than they are asking for; or that maybe the timing isn't right; it isn't good for the entire family, but that you'll seriously consider it.

Collaborate with them. Engage them in conversation. Show a keen interest in their thoughts. Value their points of view, opinions and tastes. You may not like their music, but what do you expect? You expect them to like the music you like…music they've never heard…that only geezers can appreciate? And don't insult them for their taste in music. You'll pay down the road. Besides, their taste will change anyway.

> Teach your kids that they can talk to you about anything, that their thoughts are valuable and worth hearing.

If your kids ask you to come to their room to listen to a tune on a new CD, do it. And don't trash it. Find something good to say about it, e.g., great rhythm, unique arrangement, outstanding vocals, good beat, "I can understand why you like it," "Does it ever end???"

We've covered some of this before, but in talking with your kids, don't embarrass them—ever! Don't use a threatening tone; talk more in statements rather than questions; don't always look them in the eye; don't sound like a know-it-all. Parents that try to sound like know-it-alls are simply revealing their insecurities.

Want to see your kids' self-confidence grow?
6. Teach them to achieve something, be productive, responsible, and get good results. They can learn to baby-sit, lifeguard, mow yards, look after the neighbor's dogs, rake leaves, set up a lemonade stand, sweep out the garage, wash the car, get an after-school job, work on the yearbook staff, whatever. The more kids achieve, the more reason others have opportunity to appreciate what they do and commend them for it. Competence

is at the root of self-confidence. What makes a golfer feel good about his golf game? The pro riding around with him in the golf cart bragging on his set of clubs and outfit? No. What makes him feel confident about his golf game is to gradually get better and better at putting the ball where it needs to be with a given shot! Achievement, good results, work ethic! There's nothing quite like a kid finding something he can excel at to build his self-confidence! Parents should treat it like a vein of gold to be mined and encouraged by finding opportunities for the kid to explore and improve.

Want to see your child's self-confidence improve?
7. Help her understand that God has a plan and purpose for her life, that she can achieve something good and decent and productive if she'll just stay in the groove and grow in her faith. As a believer in Christ, she's not working alone. The Apostle Paul wrote in Colossians 1:29, *This is my work, and I can do it only because Christ's mighty energy is at work within me.* Matthew 6:33 says, *and he will give you all you need from day to day if you live for him and make the Kingdom of God your primary concern.* Faith in Christ must become the cornerstone of our children's lives. Our job is to lead them to that faith in Christ by word and example.

Want to see your children's self-confidence grow?
8. Make sure they know you enjoy being around them—without crowding them—that you get a boost just from hanging with them. Children love to bring pleasure. The last thing they want is to feel is that they're a problem, a burden or an imposition. Laugh *with* them and laugh *at* them. They love to think they're entertaining you.

Want to see your kids' self-confidence blossom?
9. Make sure they know that you love your spouse and can see evidences of it in your relationship, such as holding hands, hugging, kissing, saying "I love you." Kids may say "yuk," but they're thinking, "Yes! Whew! They're not going to get a divorce." If you don't have a spouse, make sure they know that you love someone else who is special to you, e.g., Christ, your mother, father, a relative. Children need to see genuine love modeled in a godly way.

Want to see your kids' self-confidence grow? **10. Believe in them**, and prove that you believe in them by giving them space to fail as well as space to succeed. Dr. Howard Hendricks, popular author, speaker and founder of the Center for Leadership at Dallas Theological Seminary, once said, "Our research indicates that the reason most men and women never get across the threshold of success in life is that they never had anyone to believe in them." Your kids need to know that you are in their corner, that you believe in them, and that they can do something significant with their lives. In the process, just be careful not to favor one child over the other because of appearance, better grades, athleticism, or whatever. Every child is special at home. At home the ground should always be level.

Well, there they are—10 ways to improve your child's self-confidence. I hope you'll put them into practice. They'll work wonders!

discussion

1. Think back for a moment to your own upbringing. Did you feel that you had the blessing of your mother and father? If the answer is yes, what did that mean to you and how did it make you feel? If the answer is no, what do you think you missed?

_____

_____

2. In your opinion, what does it mean to "bless" your children? What are some practical ways you can bless them that they will be able to recognize and appreciate? Make some notes and discuss.

_____

_____

3. It seems that kids today are under as much pressure as their parents—sometimes more—with school, homework, organizations, sports, activities, church, social life, part-time work and the like. Is there really any time or way they can contribute to the overall benefit of the home and family? After all, is it really that important? What should the priorities be?

_____

_____

4. What can children do that will make them feel that they are actually contributing to the well being of the family? At what age should they start?

_____

_____

5. Do you feel that your kids are self-confident? Why or why not? Make some notes and discuss openly with the group.

_____

_____

6. In light of the 10 points in this lesson, can you think of some other confidence-builders that might make a difference? If so, what are they?

_____

_____

application

lifescene

(True Story) *A pastor and his wife had a young son who struggled in the area of self-confidence all through elementary school, junior high and senior high school. He was fine around everybody at church, but away from church he suffered greatly. He just didn't fit in socially and had very few friends. When he was 15, the church's music director encouraged him to join the youth choir, where he quickly realized that the boy had a gifted singing voice. He then encouraged him to begin singing in the adult choir, even though he was really too young. The director soon gave him a short solo part which he performed with ease, much to the pleasure of the congregation. Soon his parents arranged for him to take voice lessons from an outstanding voice teacher in the area. At the voice teacher's annual "Spring Serenade and Recital" at the local high school auditorium, a crowd of 1,000 people applauded his performance with a standing ovation—the only one of the evening. From that point forward, the young man was never the same again. He went on to enjoy an outstanding career as a performer, recording artist, vocal coach, and successful businessman.*

What do you think are some factors that made the difference in this young man's life and gave him the confidence to excel? How might any of this apply to your children? Make some notes and discuss as a group.

_____

_____

_____

_____

prayer

Dear Father, when I am tempted to think that simply loving my children is enough, help me to realize that real love must take action. I must bless them, think ahead of them, be perceptive, and help them find their unique place in life based on what they have to work with. Most of all, I commit to you that I will do my best to help them discover your overall plan and purpose for their lives. Therein lies true self-confidence. In Jesus' name, Amen.

— It's never too late to become a better parent. —

Caution: Danger Ahead!

Observe the Warning Signs before Tempers Flare

This is one of those topics that's not a barrel of fun to talk about, but it's one that parents desperately need to consider. I am convinced that improperly expressed anger in the home drives the wedge more deeply between parent-child relationships than any other single factor. And I honestly think it is needless.

In the title itself—CAUTION: ANGER AHEAD! —I am suggesting that anger is a normal emotion that we all have a right to express, but we need to be cautious how we express it. James 1:19 says, *Everyone should be quick to listen, slow to speak and slow to become angry, for man's anger does not bring about the righteous life that God desires.*

When you as a parent begin to feel angry at your child, watch out for these warning signs.

✱ STOP—A flag goes up in your mind; the cross bar lowers; you stop—look—listen—pause to think and gather control of yourself, trying to determine what's really going on in the situation so you don't wind up saying or doing something you'll be sorry about later. So the first warning sign is STOP. Another warning sign is . . .

✱ DETOUR—You take an alternate route to get where you're going. You choose not to strike out verbally with harsh, threatening words and tone. Instead, you take another path and find solutions to the problem at hand. When you detour and take a different direction, it may seem a little unfamiliar at first, but if you keep moving and stay on it, you will usually get back on track to a frame of mind that will allow you to resolve the issues at hand. A second warning sign we need to observe when we see anger ahead is DETOUR. If we don't observe the first two signs, we can always plow ahead and…

✱ CRASH 'N BURN—When you become angry at your child, you can throw self-control to the wind, go charging into the fray, say whatever you please however you please regardless of the feelings of the child, attacking, belittling, "putting him in his place," focusing on the character instead of the behavior, assuming that because you're the parent, what you think, say and feel is all that matters. In other words, you can crash right through the crossbar and plunge over the precipice into the torrent below. Yes, parents can do this, but over time everybody is likely to pay dearly.

In a perfect world, parents and children would learn to recognize their anger, understand what's causing it, control themselves, express their anger properly, and move on. They'd all practice Ephesians 4:26-27 that tells us that it's all right to be angry, but it's not all right for our anger to cause us to sin. We're not to *let the sun go down* while we're still angry—we're not to harbor anger over time and allow Satan to gain a foothold in our lives.

Let's talk for a moment about why *parents* become angry. We all expect certain things out of life: fairness, appreciation, agreement, and willingness to do things our way. We can feel hurt and disappointed that our expectations are not met, and often our disappointment can turn to anger. In other words, when life doesn't go according to our plans, we can become angry—we get mad. James 4:1-2 speaks to this: *What is causing the quarrels and fights among you? Don't they come from the evil desires at war within you? You want what you don't have, so you scheme…to get it.* Dr. Jerry Deffenbacher, a psychologist who specializes in anger management, says the underlying message of highly angry people, is "Things oughta go my way!"

> ## The underlying message of highly angry people is "Things oughta go my way!"

Most studies reveal the basis of all anger is fear, fear of being threatened or fear of losing control. When our kids aren't living up to our expectations, we fear what others might think of us, or we react to fear of being a failure as a parent.

Think about it for a minute. What are you afraid of? Do you realize what a huge motivator "fear" is? Some say it's the biggest motivator there is. I can assure you, though, that there one thing that's stronger than fear—and that is faith— Forsaking All I Trust Him.

What do your kids do that causes your volcano to erupt anyway? Is it possible to see it coming in time to get yourself under control? I think the

first step is to look within, and ask yourself these questions:

- When was the last time I had an angry outburst? What initiated it?
- The last time I "lost it"…were there any signs that I was on the verge of losing it? Was I feeling extra tired, hurt, frustrated, sick or tense?
- Are my expectations unreasonable?
- What am I afraid of? What am I reacting to in fear?
- Am I focusing on what has been done *to me* rather than what I *can do* for someone else?
- Is my ability to think clearly impaired when I am angry? Can I be objective?
- Does the way I express anger bring any resolution and peace, or does it just cause more hurt and damage?

Parents, let me suggest some practical steps you can take to deal with your anger.

- **Stop!** Hold everything! Be silent. Get control of yourself. Take a deep breath and let your feelings calm. Remove yourself momentarily from the situation.
- **Ask yourself: What is really going on here?** Is there some other issue that is co-fueling my feelings? Try to get a clear picture of what's really happening. Am I part of the problem here?
- **Express your anger.** Voice your feelings honestly and in a reasonable tone of voice, without attacking the child.
- **Address the behavior—not the child.** Use "I" statements instead of "you" statements, such as, "I am angry because mud is all over my front seat, and there is no appreciation for picking you up every day after school." This expression voices your frustration without accusation or blame. Most children will respond appropriately, taking responsibility for their part in your anger, i.e. "I'm sorry, I'll clean the front seat; and I'm really glad you pick me up every day after school."
- **Problem-solve.** Ask your child for input when trying to resolve a conflict such as, "How do you think we could have avoided the unpleasant experience on the way home from school today?"
- **Express pleasure** when the child changes his behavior.

Now let's think about why *children* get angry. Sometimes parents write off a child's anger as "just the way he is" and allow their child to control them with his anger. But parents can fuel anger in their children without realizing it. Some of the reasons children become angry are:

- *Frustration*—Sometimes they are pushed or provoked into a state of frustration. Ephesians 6:4 says, *Fathers, do not provoke your children to anger by the way you treat them.* Frustration and exasperation can be caused by . . .
- *Impatience*—A constant attitude of impatience toward your child makes him feel he is in your way and never meets your expectations.
- *Inconsistency*—Inconsistency in parental supervision, discipline or rules is very frustrating to a child. Children feel confused when boundaries are constantly changing.
- *Fear*—Fear of rejection or abandonment and fear of failure often manifest themselves as anger. Some children internalize pressure to excel in academics or sports.
- *Modeling*—A child's anger can come from acting out what he sees in his family. Whether subtly or blatantly, we can model anger to our child. Just as children learn to walk and talk by watching us, so they will learn to imitate our anger. Kids learn from our good examples and our bad examples.
- *Birth Order*—A number of middle children exhibit anger about their place in the lineup of offspring. Also, anger can develop within a child who feels *less* intelligent, *not* as physically capable or *less* talented than an older sibling. Parents must give careful attention to these issues.

Concerning anger in children, our goal is not to repress or eliminate angry feelings in children – or in ourselves – but rather to accept the feelings and direct them to constructive ends. Obviously, excessive or recurrent anger on the part of parents or children can indicate deeper problems that may require professional counseling.

Finally, let me suggest a couple of effective ways to teach responsibility and anger management skills to your children.

First, **Responsibility = Choices + Consequences.** Responsibility is learned by making choices, following through, and then accepting the outcome and consequences of those choices and decisions. Children need to understand that every decision is a choice. "If you choose to throw books across the room, you have chosen to clean up the mess, as well as the consequences of no TV, no computer and no telephone. It's your choice." Still, however, they must learn that throwing books across the room is unacceptable behavior.

> *Example* is not just the *best* way to teach anger management— it's the *only* way!

Second, by **personal example.** Some authorities think that *example* is not just the *best* way to teach character and anger management to our children—it's the *only* way! The way you manage your anger and frustration provides children with the best possible model of handling their own.

When you see the warning signs that anger is brewing, just remember—anger is a feeling, and behavior is a choice. So choose wisely—choose patience, understanding, resolution and forgiveness, and choose to live in harmony with those you love the most.

discussion

1. Let's consider James 1:19 for a moment. What do these phrases suggest to you as a parent?

Quick to listen - _____

Slow to speak - _____

Slow to become angry - _____

The second half of the verse is "…*for man's anger does not bring about the righteous life that God desires.*" What is it about anger that can hurt us and prevent us from enjoying the life that God wants for us?

_____

_____

2. As parents, we find ourselves in all kind of situations where we can become frustrated and angry. List three or four potential anger moments that you routinely encounter with your child. Discuss as a group.

_____

_____

_____

3. Given the possibilities, what would you say angers you the most in dealing with your kids? Sibling rivalry, disobedience, laziness, talking back, disrespect, messiness, etc.? Share openly as a group.

_____

4. Which of these age groups do you think are more likely to cause parents to become angry? How would you rank them (#1 highest, #6 lowest)

____Babies ____Toddlers ____ Preschoolers ____ Elementary ____Junior High ____High School?

Where in this range of ages should parents begin to be extra careful as to how they express their anger?

_____

5. Anger between two individuals can be extremely divisive, temporarily and over time. Who do you think is in the strongest position to drive the wedge between the parent-child relationship when it comes to how anger is expressed? The parent or the child? Why do you think so? What happens? Discuss as a group.

_____

_____

6. Do you think a parent is ever justified to absolutely go over the edge and completely lose control? Why or why not? What are the consequences likely to be?

_____

_____

7. Do you agree with the following statement: *Anger is a feeling—behavior is a choice.* Why or why not? Discuss.

_____

_____

8. Complete the following sentence with your own thoughts: Even though we all have different personalities and different ways of expressing ourselves, when we become angry, we do not

_____

_____

On the other hand, when we see the caution sign and sense that there's anger ahead, we must first

and foremost exercise self-control and_____

_____

application

lifescene

Martin and Katie have a reputation for being two of the most tolerant, laid back parents you'd ever meet. Nothing their kids do in public seems to bother them. Late one night in the grocery store, Katie is trying to help her 4-year old Amanda understand that she has to stay in the child seat of the grocery cart…that they're not going down the candy isle tonight. Amanda stiffens up, talks back to her mother and takes a swat at her, knocking her glasses off and popping a lens out. Without thinking, Katie slaps Amanda sharply on the cheek, leaving a clear handprint. Amanda is crying at the top of her voice, "You're hitting me! That hurt!" A friend from church hears the child, rounds the corner and sees the commotion. She hurriedly walks over and says, "Oh my, Katie, look at her face! Poor…..!" Realizing what she has just heard and seen, the friend quietly walks away with Amanda howling in the background. Katie's hands are trembling as she tries to put the lens back in her glasses.

If you had been Katie's friend from church, what would you have done in this situation? What happened to Katie? How should she have handled Amanda? What about Katie's friend? Should Katie call her, try to justify her anger and explain things? Make some notes and discuss what you think is going on here.

_____

_____

_____

_____

prayer

Dear Father, I have come to know that anger is a part of life. You have given us this emotion for self-preservation and to express extreme displeasure. Sometimes we need to be angry…but *good* and angry—not bad and angry! Please help me to STOP when I see the warning signs and DETOUR around the chasm where tempers flare and feelings are damaged. Above all, help me to realize that I have all of the patience and love and self-control I need right here at my disposal because your Holy Spirit is alive within me. Help me to see your warning flag go up, so I can cautiously choose a firm but kinder path to the peaceful resolution of the conflicts that life brings.

— It's never too late to become a better parent. —

Birth Order – And What You Need to Know About It

Recognize Your Children's Differences and Turn Them into Advantages

key scripture

You made all the delicate, inner parts of my body and knit me together in my mother's womb. Thank you for making me so wonderfully complex! Your workmanship is marvelous—and how well I know it.

Psalm 139:13-14

One reason I love this topic is because it encapsulates so much of what we've already talked about—including the importance of recognizing the individuality of each of your children. That's really what birth order is all about. And here's a guarantee you can count on—If your first child turns right, your second one will turn left, your third one may go up and over!

Most people don't give much thought to the sequence in which their children are born, but they really should because birth order speaks of the majesty and wonder of God. One of life's great mysteries is how these "little cubs can all come out of the same den" with the same mother and father, and yet be so different. That's the wonder of it all—realizing that God has made each of us to unique.

Our key scripture, Psalm 139:13-14, says, *You made all the delicate, inner parts of my body and knit me together in my mother's womb. Thank you for making me so wonderfully complex! Your workmanship is marvelous – and how well I know it.*

A baby's view of life begins to take shape the moment he arrives on the scene. How does this happen? Well, think about it. When the firstborn comes home, who are her role models? Parents—adults. And that new baby is the parents' "guinea pig." They're going to learn the ropes of parenting with this first child, responding to every cry immediately, planning every detail of the baby's day. As she gets older that firstborn develops a need to know exactly what her day holds in store. She doesn't like surprises. When she asks, "What time are we leaving?"…you don't answer "Somewhere around 9:30'ish." She wants you to be a little more specific than that.

Think back to the way you documented every move in your first baby's life. You've got a dozen photo albums, carefully chronicled, to prove your dedication, while the next two kids are lucky to rate a shoebox of random photos. What's interesting is that the firstborn child models the conscientious traits of the parents. He or she is orderly, a list maker, and comes to expect that his or her needs will be met with certainty and swiftness.

Firstborn children are groomed for success. They are leaders who learn to dominate their surroundings because they go unchallenged within the first few years of life. Consider this: Of the first 23 astronauts in our space program, 21 were firstborn children. The other two were "only" children. The fact is, your first child has just about everything going for him—that is, until he hears some news around the house—"Guess what, Joe Bob! You're going to have a baby sister."

When we look into the newborn face of that *second child*, we automatically think, "Hey, this baby doesn't look at all like the first one!" Well, should he? People just seem to expect a replica of the first child. When teachers are checking roll on the first day of school and see the last name of a kid they had before, they may be elated—or terrified—to think that the same mold has surfaced a second time. But, of course, most teachers know better.

When the *middle child* comes home, the firstborn wonders why this little bundle of trouble has invaded his territory, and sibling rivalry begins in earnest as two kids are now in competition for the parent's attention. The wise parent will go to that older child and point out things such as, "Look at that baby, can he walk?" "No," he'll say. "But you *can* walk. And how many naps do you take a day?" "One," the older child will say. "Think about how many naps the new baby has to take – eight!" "See, you're the big brother now; and you're going to get to help your little brother grow up. Maybe you can teach him how to do some of the things you can do—like choke the dog and dump out the goldfish!" Seriously, you want to affirm your older child and his position with relation to the younger child.

As soon as the *middle child* starts to crawl, he lands in the middle of big brother's stuff. He's the rough and tumble competitor who realizes that when he wants certain toys to play with, taking them away from big brother seems like the best option. And he will use those toys in a way that never occurred to the older child. In a word, middle children tend to march to the beat of a different drummer, and they are more likely to be strong-willed and rebellious. Statistics show that they have a tendency toward becoming entrepreneurs. Some of today's most successful business innovators are middle children. From biblical characters such as Cain and Abel to some recent U.S. presidents and their brothers, history shows the firstborn and second child will see life through a different lens. And to further complicate matters, the parents once again announce, "We're having another baby!"

Well, this *last-born* of the family— Little Schnooky, as I like to call him—goes through life looking *up*! He must figure out how to get attention over and above the shenanigans of the older kids. But this youngster is likely to be the most social of the bunch, never meeting a stranger. He becomes adept at being manipulative and jumping into situations with both feet and asking questions later. Research shows that youngest children are top salesmen, and many times turn out to be the comedians of the family. Some of America's most popular comedians are babies of their families who capitalized on their ability to entertain and make people laugh.

Have you ever had the feeling that you should treat all of your children the same? Whether you live in Arizona, Texas or Virginia, the state you live in will treat your 16-year old a little different from the way it treats your 14-year old. Life treats people differently, according to where they are in the progression of life. As parents, we don't need to be afraid to treat our children differently concerning curfews, bed times, allowances, chores, TV and computer time, cell phone privileges, driving the car and the like. Core beliefs, values, principles of right and wrong remain consistent, but privileges should vary according to age and maturity. Whenever possible, some of the chores of the older children should be passed down to the younger children as older kids' lives become more complicated and they are granted more independence for making their own decisions.

> God designed each of us to be unique, with our own personality, interests, appearance and potential.

Ask yourself this question: Does God give us all the same gifts to work with in life? Does he expect the exact same thing of all of us? No. He designed each of us to be unique, with our own personality, abilities, interests, appearance and potential. In Jeremiah 1:5, the Lord says, *I knew you before I formed you in your mother's womb. Before you were born, I set you apart….* Matt. 10:30 says, *And the very hairs of your head are all numbered.*

Knowing that each child is distinctive gives parents an opportunity to point out that God has a plan that is specific to each child. Does God expect us to meet the same standard when we come to faith in Christ, to learn and practice godly values, to live obediently to his Word? Yes. But one of the great privileges of parenting is the opportunity we have to recognize our children's distinct differences and turn them into advantages—showing absolutely no favoritism to which one happens to be the smartest, the best athlete, or the most attractive!

> God made us, and we should praise him for making each member of our family so wonderfully different and complex.

Let me give you three variables that will have a profound effect on birth order:

- **Sex of the children** – If you have two girls and then have a son, he will generally display the traits of the firstborn child.

- **Physical characteristics** – When the younger children are physically bigger and taller then the older child, the older child may submit to their leadership rather than try to lead them.

- **Critical eye** – Here is a variable that can do a lot of damage. Parents with an overly critical eye—I call them *flawpickers*—tend to find some little something wrong with everything a child does. Parents who pick at the flaws of the firstborn child may very well wind up with a kid who is unreliable, unconscientious, or maybe even a "slob" who never gets anything done, much less done right. Why? Because he's so afraid he'll be criticized. He's already accustomed to being picked to pieces! In his mind, he'll say "I'll just make a practice of not finishing things. That way I can't possibly be criticized." Parents, the lesson is—if you're a *flawpicker*, there's a good chance you'll raise a kid who's going to go through life putting himself down.

Are we trying to raise perfect kids? No. The goal is not to raise a kid who is a pursuer of perfection, but a pursuer of excellence. A perfectionist sets up standards in which he is bound to fail. It has been said that "perfectionism is a slow way to die." You're bound to fail somewhere along the way. On this earth you can't achieve perfection! And even if you could, no one would recognize it because no one has seen it before! The pursuer of excellence, on the other hand, has high standards, and he tries hard to reach them. There's a huge difference here. One way to determine which of these you are as a parent is to ask yourself how you respond to criticism. The pursuer of excellence welcomes criticism, is not threatened, is open to suggestions, and feels better equipped to achieve his goals. When the perfectionist is criticized or fails, he often simply shuts down, feeling frustrated and disappointed in himself.

Here are some more things you need to know about birth order that will help you raise rock-solid kids.

- *First-born* – Remember, first-borns need to know specifics. Don't give them too much responsibility for their age, or they will "skip" childhood altogether. Be careful about over-correcting or micro-managing them. If you turn them into perfectionists, you'll end up with kids who will feel defeated at every turn. Also, be careful not to "should" your firstborn. Don't say "you *should* do this, you *should* do that." In other words, what they're doing is never enough. Instead, project just the opposite—"I love you just the way you are."

- *Middle child* – Middle children need to be listened to! Ask their opinion about anything, e.g., vacation planning, décor, purchases, etc. Take two-on-one time, where both mom and dad get the middle child. Look for exclusive territory, even if it's "Honey, why don't you pick the restaurant?" Let the middle child know, "Hey, we respect you as an individual." If you do, you'll neutralize some of the competitive spirit that is naturally present.

- **Baby of the family** – Last-borns need to be given the opportunity to lead, perhaps in family outings or in planning celebrations. The baby of the family will have much to compare himself to, so affirmation is crucial. If they feel less academic or less athletic than their older siblings, help them identify and develop their own unique strengths. Enjoy their social skills, laugh *with* them and *at* them as they entertain you, and remind them that every gift of life is God-given.

Only-children are in a class by themselves. By the time they're in the second grade, age 7 or 8, they function as pint-sized adults. The secret here is not to let these kids get too far ahead of themselves.

Another intriguing combination of children is *identical twins*. Why God created two kids out of the same DNA but gave them different fingerprints, I'll never know! I guess it's his way of saying, "You may look just like your sister, but there's really no one else like you." People spend billions of dollars every year trying to be like and look like other people. But no matter how many resources they have, they are uniquely themselves. It's when they artificially try to "be" someone else that trouble begins.

Well, there you are. A few things you need to know about birth order. Just remember, you and I and our kids are *who* God made us to be, and we should praise him for making each member of our family so wonderfully different and complex. His workmanship is marvelous and never ceases to amaze me! Do we have room to grow and develop? Yes. Do we have the responsibility to help our kids grow and develop and mature into healthy, well-adjusted members of society? Yes. But in so doing, I just hope you'll teach your kids the joy of being a *one-of-a-kind creation* of God who has your attention and blessing. Whether they are the first-born, middle child, last child or something in between, let each one know that he or she is truly special to you! And that you'll always be their #1 fan!

discussion

1. Psalm 139:13-14 says, *You made all the delicate, inner parts of my body and knit me together in my mother's womb. Thank you for making me so wonderfully complex! Your workmanship is marvelous – and how well I know it.* What does this verse say to you about the differences in each of us? Do you think most children and adults see their differences as "marvelous"? How can you use this verse to help children see their differences as advantages?

_____

_____

2. As kids grow and develop, sometimes they struggle with their differences. As parents, we sometimes wrestle with the fact that their personalities, tastes and characteristics are so varied. How about the home you were raised in? Did you notice any differences between yourself and your siblings that were challenging to you and your parents? How did it all get resolved? Make some notes and discuss together.

_____

_____

3. After studying the differences in children due to birth order, how would you describe the differences between you and your spouse in terms of what each of you brings to the marriage to balance each other? Which of your individual traits bring diverse perspectives on parenting? Are you able to blend your differences into harmony, or do they result in discord?

_____

_____

4. According to the video lesson, when does sibling rivalry begin? What can parents do immediately to reassure the firstborn in the family so he or she doesn't need to feel set aside or deserted?

_____

_____

5. Understanding the characteristics of birth order prepares us to recognize our children's differences and turn them into advantages. Beside each descriptive word below, write a 1, 2, or 3 to indicate whether that word is applicable to the first-born, middle child or baby of the family.

_____ Manipulative	_____ Leader	_____ Comedian
_____ Great Communicator	_____ Entrepreneur	_____ Adult-like
_____ Rough & Tumble	_____ Dominates	_____ Follows rules

6. Regardless of birth order, we must recognize that God loves each of us the same, while at the same time he has given us different abilities and personality traits to work with in life. As a group, share a few of the unique qualities you recognize in your children and how these qualities can contribute to a successful, productive life in the future. Make a few notes.

_____

_____

application

lifescene

Jason Carrington is a 16 year old young man who appears to be average to below average in most every category that kids recognize. He's ordinary looking, not athletically gifted enough to make any of the teams he has tried out for, a little quiet, and makes OK grades even though he studies hard and always turns his material in on time. His face stays broken out most of the time, and he's a little embarrassed by it. He thinks that's maybe one reason girls don't seem interested in him, although he is interested in them. What Jason will do, however, is work. Hard. And he takes his church life seriously, volunteering to help out wherever he is needed. His dad makes him a loan of $750 to buy some lawn equipment and then challenges him to go get some customers, do excellent and dependable work, <u>make</u> some money, <u>manage</u> it and <u>multiply</u> it. Before long, Jason is making more money than anybody in his school. He spends a little, saves a lot, and invests the rest in more equipment and a used pick-up truck and trailer so he can hire some of his fellow students who have asked to come to work for him. Now he has time to get more customers and supervise his guys, making sure they do top quality work in a timely manner. He maintains his landscape business year round, and the same guys that started with him are still with him when he enters his senior year in high school. He now has ten guys working for him, lots of equipment, money in the bank, and a waiting list of potential customers, some of them commercial ones who are willing to pay top dollar for his level of work.

Suppose you are the mother of a cute 18-year old daughter, and you've followed John's business career from the start, watching him take care of your lawn. What might you be thinking and why? Do you think Jason is a first-born, middle child, last-born or only child? What do you think are some factors that have made the difference in his life, and what do you think the future holds for a kid like Jason Carrington?

_____

_____

_____

_____

prayer

Dear Father, thank you for the life and potential you have placed in each of us. Thank you for giving us varied abilities and characteristics that we can use to contribute to your kingdom. Thank you that we are all different, that my children are all different, so we can marvel at how your will and work is fulfilled through our lives. Help us to realize that one of our jobs as parents is to help our children understand that they are designed to be a vital part of your Body, the Body of Christ, so they can carry out your plan and purpose in the world. In Jesus' name, Amen.

— It's never too late to become a better parent. —

Standing Up to the New Goliath

Helping Kids Overcome the Negative Influence of the Internet, the Media and Technology

One of the most compelling stories in all the Bible is the story of David and Goliath found in 1 Samuel 17. Let's relive the story for a moment.

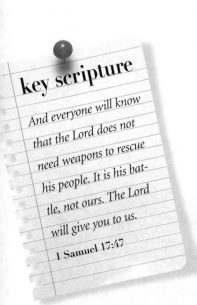

For 40 days, the Philistines and the Israelites have been facing each other on opposite hills with the Valley of Elah between them. Goliath shouts across to the Israelites, *Do you need a whole army to settle this? Choose someone to fight for you and it will represent the Philistines. We will settle this dispute in simple combat! If your man is able to kill me, then we will be your slaves. But if I kill him, you will be our slaves! I defy the armies of Israel! Send me a man who will fight with me!* You can imagine the fear in the hearts of the Israelites!

The fact is, in early biblical times, an army often avoided the high cost of human life in battle by pitting its strongest warrior against the strongest warrior of the enemy. This avoided great bloodshed because the winner of the fight was considered the winner of the battle.

Goliath had the definite advantage against David from a human standpoint. But Goliath didn't realize that in fighting David, he also was fighting God!

Ever wonder what Goliath looked like? Well, you saw a life-sized statue of him in the video lesson. He was around 9 ½ feet tall; probably weighed 400 pounds; his coat of mail weighed 125 pounds, and the tip of his spear weighed 15 pounds! This is one big, bad boy!

About the same time Goliath is shouting his challenge to the Israelites, a young shepherd boy from Bethlehem by the name of David is taking some food out to his brothers who are with the Israelite army. David starts asking questions about who this big guy is that's taunting and defying the armies of God! Nobody takes him seriously, though. They basically tell him to go back to minding his sheep.

Then David says to King Saul in verse 32, "Don't worry about a thing; I'll go fight this Philistine!" Well, you know the rest. David picks up five smooth stones from a stream bed…puts them in his bag…and armed only with his shepherd's staff and sling, starts across to fight Goliath. Goliath "walks" out to meet David, but David "runs" out to meet Goliath. David hits Goliath in the forehead with one stone, and Goliath falls to the ground—out cold! Since David had nothing but the sling and five stones, verse 51 tells us that he took Goliath's own sword and killed him with it, then cut off his head and took it to King Saul. Curious as to who this kid was, Saul said to David, "Tell me about your father, my boy." There in the shadow of the dead giant, David humbly replied, "My father's name is Jesse, and we live in Bethlehem."

What Goliath didn't understand as he was taunting this young man with threats of a quick defeat was that he was not just fighting a young shepherd boy—he was fighting God himself.

Parents, our kids are facing another giant today—one that I call the "new Goliath"—and it's out there tempting, enticing, and taunting our kids to come jump into the fray, throw morals, Christian values and beliefs out the door, and go for all the pleasure they can find! And this new Goliath consists of the "Internet," the "media," and "technology." I hope you agree that we can't stand on the sidelines and let our kids fight alone.

So here's my question for you: How are your kids going to stand up to this new Goliath? What are you packing in their bag that they can use—today!—to overcome the negative influence of this 21st century giant?

You see, our goal is not to overcome the Internet, the media, and technology, but to overcome their *negative influences*, all the while using them in a positive way to benefit our way of life. Here are some suggestions for helping our kids stand up to the new Goliath.

First, let's talk about the INTERNET.

When I was growing up, I still remember pacing the floor waiting on mom to get off our only phone line, so I could call a buddy. If we wanted to get a group together to play baseball, we each had to call one kid, and ask him to call one, and so on. Since the phone was in the kitchen – conversations were public family knowledge.

Today, kids can use the Internet to talk to 50 of their most intimate friends; and hundreds they don't even know – the second they post a message on MySpace. Over the Internet, they can be in constant contact with each other – and all conversation is private. Yes, the world has changed since my day!

The ironic thing about Internet access—and cell phones, for that matter—is that your child is isolated from you while at the same being "connected to the universe." Because it's such a private thing, a natural gap can widen between us, our kids, and their social lives.

Let me suggest a few things you should implement when you feel that your child is ready to join the world of cyberspace.

Be informed – know what's out there. Most parents know only a fraction of what their kids know about "their world" on the Internet. Hone in on articles in newspapers, magazines and the Internet that relate to trends, new products and services that appeal to kids. Nationally-respected organizations publish watchdog material to keep parents informed and ahead of the game. Kids are surprised – and actually impressed – when parents know more than they do about trendy techno stuff. Sometimes, just the parents' awareness is enough to put the kid on notice.

Lay down some ground rules concerning use of the computer. Educate the child a bit; talk about what's out there, and where the landmines are that kids can step on. If the kid is more computer literate that you are, at least learn enough to establish the boundaries, and if the kid chooses to break the agreed-upon rules, he is at the same time choosing the consequences. And assure him that he won't like them.

Keep the computer in a common room in the house until you feel that you can trust your child. He should be aware that anyone in the family may walk up at any time. Do not put the computer in the child's bedroom initially.

> Our goal is not to overcome the Internet, but to overcome it's *negative influences.*

Make sure you are "computer savvy" and that your kids are going to become "computer savvy." Tell them that whatever they are told online may or may not be true, not to give out personal information to strangers, and not to respond to suggestive postings. Remind kids there is no such thing as anonymity, and to expect what they say on the Internet, including chat rooms, to be made public. Tell your kids to report cyber-bullying or any inappropriate emails directed toward them personally.

Know your child's passwords and randomly check their email. Tell them you will monitor their activity on the Internet, and give them the reasons why. Then do some non-threatening probing. No one likes to have someone walk up behind them and stare at their private conversations, but you should be able to walk by and ask, "Anything interesting on the Internet?" "You're careful with what you open, aren't you." "Who are you talking to?" "What's up with them?" "What do you two have planned?" Note your child's reactions, and sense whether there should be cause for concern.

> Remind kids there is no such thing as anonymity, and to expect what they say on the Internet to be made public.

Jump in. Recognizing MySpace as the venue that millions of kids were using, I went to the site and "jumped in." I went through the motions of setting up my own account. After filling in the requested blanks, I was invited (in small print) to review the privacy policy. Look at an excerpt:

Privacy policy for MySpace: *To enrich our members' experience, we request and display some <u>personal information</u> to other members and <u>visitors</u>, which allows our users to identify each other and expand their network of friends.*

The privacy policy goes on to say that notifications are sent to users with your first and last name, email address, age, personal interests, gender, education and occupation – to assist them in finding and communicating with you. It further states that your profile information, including your IP address may be shared with third parties for more relevant services and advertisements to members. Now I ask you, does anything about that sound private?

The new account immediately asks you to list your school. A child quickly learns that he is missing out if he's not on the network with the kids at school. That's the in-crowd. So, now his conversations and profile are open to other students in school; and their friends, and their friends' friends, whether he knows them or not. They post pictures and special interests which attract curious and like-minded kids from all over the country. Anyone can set up a MySpace account within a couple of minutes. Once in, you have intimate access to kids never before within your reach. Kids will say things on the Internet they would never say in person.

To say that Internet pornography is rampant is an understatement! It's a multi-billion dollar industry. An email or web site can be opened innocently, and pop-ups can start appearing on the computer to the extent that your computer is taken captive by them. It's near impossible to get rid of pop-ups! Small children can open an email innocently and see images they will never forget! Certain "Peer-to-Peer" programs—called P2P—can download explicit content that cannot be blocked by some Internet filters.

But! There is good news! Hopefully, you've already heard of BSAFE, a popular and powerful Internet filter that is endorsed by many Christian organizations. It blocks pop-ups, bad advertising images, questionable web sites so that it won't even allow your computer to load them. If you don't have BSAFE, you should get it! It's pronounced "be-safe"!

Another safeguard program you should consider is Max Predator Guard. Max will:

- Protect children from dangers that parental controls do not!
- Protect your children from dangers associated with peer-to-peer networks, instant messaging, chat and websites such as MySpace!
- Record ALL instant messaging and chat room

conversations of your children while using MSN, AOL, Yahoo, and Triton!
- Work with ALL high-speed, wireless and dial-up services!

Why do we need these safeguards? Because the Internet provides an open season for sexual predators. There are over one million sexual predators and pedophiles who surf the Internet everyday, looking for children and teens they can sexually seduce, both emotionally and physically. You are the key to your family's protection, and revolutionary new tools like BSAFE and Max Predator Guard will enable you to protect your children like never before.

How could a child be persuaded to meet with a stranger? These individuals will target a hobby or skill posted by your child on his profile. They will then strike up a relationship based on common interest. Predators stay up on the latest music kids listen to and the most popular TV shows among young people.

Those that prey on children are persistent. They will be attentive and complimentary. Your child may receive gifts in the mail or cards with money. Once the child admits even the most minor conflict with his parents, the stranger will embrace him and take his side. He becomes your child's confidante. As the child loses any hesitation about this 'loving' new friend – the stranger begins suggesting they get together. Instant messaging, chat rooms, and the like provide predators an opportunity to monitor and try to meet child victims and take advantage of them.

What can you do to minimize the chances of an online predator victimizing your child? The FBI says:

- Communicate and talk to your child about sexual victimization and potential on-line danger.
- Spend time with your children online. Have them show you their favorite online destinations.
- Keep the computer in a common room in the house, not in your child's bedroom. It is much more difficult for a computer-sex offender to communicate with a child when the computer screen is visible to a parent or another member of the household.
- Utilize parental controls provided by your service provider and/or blocking software. While you should utilize these mechanisms, you shouldn't totally rely on them.
- Always maintain access to your child's online account and randomly check his or her email. Be aware that your child could be contacted through the U.S. Mail. Be up front with your kids about your access and reasons why.
- Teach your child the responsible use of the resources online. There is much more to the online experience than chat rooms.
- Find out what computer safeguards are used by your child's school, the public library, and the homes of your child's friends. These are all places, outside your normal supervision, where your child could encounter an online predator.
- Understand, even if your child (under 18) was a willing participant in any form of sexual exploitation, that he/she has done wrong, but is nevertheless considered the *victim*. The offender always bears the complete legal responsibility for the crime.

Instruct your children:

- To never arrange a face-to-face meeting with someone they met online.
- To never upload (post) pictures of themselves on the Internet or online service to people they do not personally know.
- To never give out identifying information such as their name, home address, school name, or telephone number.
- To never download pictures from an unknown source, since there is a good chance there could be sexually-explicit images involved.
- To never respond to messages or bulletin board postings that are suggestive, obscene, belligerent, or harassing.
- That whatever they are told online may or may not be true.

> Utilize parental controls provided by your service provider and/or blocking software.

The FBI has published a list of warning signs that your child might be at risk online. Measure your child's activity against these concerns:

- Your child spends large amounts of time online, especially at night.
- Your child is making or receiving phone calls from people you don't know, and numbers you don't recognize.
- Your child receives mail, gifts, or packages from someone you don't know.
- Your child turns the computer monitor off or quickly changes the screen on the monitor when you come into the room.
- Your child becomes withdrawn from the family.
- You find pornography on your child's computer.
- Your child is using an online account belonging to someone else.

Should any of the following situations arise in your household via the Internet or online service, you should immediately contact your local or state law enforcement agency, the FBI, or even the National Center for Missing and exploited Children:

- Your child or anyone in the household has received child pornography.
- Your child has been sexually solicited by someone who knows that your child is under 18 years of age.
- Your child has received sexually explicit images from someone that knows your child is under the age of 18.

Monitor your child's access to all types of live electronic communications.

Here's an important question: What do you do when you have reason to believe or, in fact, discover that your son or daughter is making improper use of the computer, visiting harmful web sites, exchanging inappropriate emails, or communicating with a sexual predator online? Here are ten suggestions:

1. Consider talking openly with your child about your suspicions. Remind him of the dangers of computer sex offenders.
2. Review what is on your child's computer. If you don't know how, ask a friend, coworker, relative or other knowledgeable person.
3. If the telephone is used, use Caller ID to determine who is calling your child. Most telephone companies that offer Caller ID also offer a service that allows you to block your number from appearing on someone else's Caller ID. Telephone companies also offer an additional service feature that rejects incoming calls that you block. Devices can be purchased that show telephone numbers that have been dialed from your home phone. Additionally, the last number called from your home phone can be retrieved provided the telephone is equipped with a redial feature.
4. Monitor your child's access to all types of live electronic communications, i.e., chat rooms, instant messages, Internet Relay Chat, etc., and monitor your child's email. Computer sex offenders almost always meet potential victims via chat rooms. After meeting a child online, they will continue to communicate electronically, often via email.
5. When it's time to confront your child, don't go storming his room and unplug his computer! In fact, do nothing until you've thought the situation through carefully and collaborated with your spouse or a trusted friend.
6. Ask yourself, "Why is he doing this? Have we as parents dropped the ball somewhere? What is our responsibility here?" The last thing you want to do is dress him down, humiliate him, and drive him away from you. Kids are curious by nature, so don't write them off and treat them like outcasts the first time you discover they've been dealing with something inappropriate on the Internet. But if it's a serious situation, treat it in a serious way!
7. How can you confront your child in as non-threatening a way as possible and help him see that this kind of activity can only hurt him instead of help him? When you do confront him, keep your voice calm, level, and concerned, but empty of emotion. Don't sound accusatory and don't glare at him in the eyes or stare him down. In fact, give him some space, and he'll be more apt to tell you the truth.

8. Appear puzzled as to why he, of all people, would be doing this. Let him know that it is unacceptable, not permitted, and if it happens again, he will lose computer privileges or more. If it does happen again, ask him if he remembers what the agreed-upon consequences would be. Follow through by removing the computer or blocking out certain uses of it. Tell him to notify you when he thinks he can and will use it properly, and you will be glad to discuss the possibility with him at that time.

9. How should your child feel when confronted? He should feel that he has disappointed you, that you are hurt, that your trust has been violated, and that he will have to regain that trust.

10. If your child has been violated by a criminal act, report it to the proper authorities.

Let me again remind you: The Internet is *not* our enemy. It is a remarkable resource that can benefit our way of life enormously! It is the negative influence and improper use of the Internet that is our enemy!

Let's talk about the MEDIA. Media may not be a four-letter word, but it gets five stars when it comes to getting your kids' attention and influencing them.

Take video games, for instance. Kids use Sony Play Stations, Microsoft X-Box, and Nintendo to play games that contain unbelievable violence, explicit material, immoral dress and conduct, red light districts, and more. The games transform players into criminals performing criminal acts. Second Life Online—a popular online role-playing game—exposes kids to advanced aspects of real life so they can act out whatever roles they wish.

What about mobile PCs and cell phones? Kids are using this technology to transfer files, programs, images, whatever…wirelessly from device to device anywhere and anytime… at school, at home, at parties, malls, etc. In other words, "your information is my information…instantly."

What does the media teach kids about sex, marriage, and having kids? That it's okay and desirable not to marry before you have kids. It's okay to live with each other before marriage…okay to move from partner to partner…okay for gays/lesbians to marry and have kids or adopt babies. There is no moral compass, and this is what our kids read and see via the media everyday!

Music and music videos reinforce these themes. Kids are taught to take their appearance to shocking levels and be creatively risqué with dance moves. The words to songs rev up their emotions – inciting thoughts of bazaar behavior.

Teen magazines exploit shocking behavior in such a way that promotes envy. Kids note what it takes to become famous and make money, then they try to imitate the behavior of their teen idols.

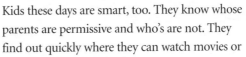

Kids these days are smart, too. They know whose parents are permissive and who's are not. They find out quickly where they can watch movies or participate in behavior that is not permitted in their own house. My suggestion is that you invite your kids to bring their friends to your house and make them feel welcome. Make your house the hangout. Be there, be available, know what's going on. Just stay out of the way.

> Invite your kids to bring their friends to your house and make them feel welcome.

When it comes to the dangers of outside influences, preventive care is priceless. With the Internet, the media and a host of other influential forces arousing their curiosity, it is imperative that we are alert and tuned in to our kids. It just requires the basics: time, attention and conversation. Your kids are worth it!

Now let's think for a moment about TECHNOLOGY. If we could see today what is going to be available in technology just five years from now, it would be mind-boggling! *Ten* years down the road, it would be unfathomable!

You can rest assured that five years from now many of the devices we are using today will be obsolete and unavailable. We won't even be using much of the terminology we're using today. New products, procedures, and market demands are going to bring people closer together. As Thomas Friedman says in his book THE WORLD IS FLAT, people no longer live on the other side of the world—they live next door. In many of the fast food restaurants you drive through, the person you hear asking for your order may be located in India—carefully coached with certain phrases so as not to sound too "foreign." He or she takes your order in India, inputs it into a computer, then sends it to the kitchen of the restaurant in America where you are waiting outside at the drive-in window. People are no longer far away—they're next door to us—or waiting inside our computer! The world is *flat!*

Anchor your kids in God's Word.

You will literally carry access to much of the world's population, news, education, information, music and entertainment in your computer phone device! In fact, you may even have a computer chip embedded permanently under your skin that recognizes your voice commands and hooks you up to people and information with no external device needed. It may even be programmed to read your thoughts, emotions, and needs, answer your questions, give you map directions, help you make decisions, and guide you through your daily schedule.

So just remember, if your kids have the latest technology, not only do they have access to millions of people around the world, those millions of people have access to your kids! And some of them are not very nice.

The focus of our session is STANDING UP TO THE NEW GOLIATH. He's big, he's powerful; he's not growing weaker with age—he's growing stronger, faster, smarter, more flexible with each week and month that passes. The question is: How are you going to help your kids overcome the negative influence of the Internet, the media, and technology now and during the coming years? In summary, here's how:

- You're going to get your head out of the sand.
- You're going to listen to your kids so you can know them better, what they're thinking, who they're running with, and what they're doing!
- You're going to become informed as to what's out there in Goliath's world, and know as much or more than your kids know.
- You're going to have some guidelines, boundaries, and expectations, and let your kids know that when they choose negative behavior, they are automatically choosing negative, unpleasant consequences. The two run parallel.
- You're going to "inspect" what you "expect." If you find violations, you're going to "disconnect" the kid, and let him "reflect" until you and he feel it is time for him to "reconnect!" **I repeat: when your child chooses negative behavior, he or she is also choosing the negative consequence that goes with it.** They come as a package! And the choice belongs to the child.
- You're going to let your kids know that adhering to your guidelines and expectations will be appreciated, valued and rewarded with greater freedom and independence. They need to learn that being a rock-solid kid has its advantages, while conforming to the pleasure-driven world is a dead-end.
- You're going to anchor your kids in God's Word, a Christian home, godly values and beliefs, and a church family where they can grow alongside other Christians.
- You're going to be a parent who sets a proper example for your kids.

Can your kids stand up to the new Goliath? Can they overcome the negative influence of the Internet, the media and technology, and at the same time use them in positive, beneficial ways? You bet they can! Millions of great kids are doing it every day! Practice "value-packed parenting," and yours will, too!

After all, Goliath was brought down by a kid. All the kid needed was a little help.

discussion

1. Were you aware of any Internet guard resources prior to participating in this lesson? If so, write them down in the space below. If they are different from the ones listed above, share them with the group

    _____

    _____

2. Have you had any personal experience in your home or acquaintance's home of a child becoming involved in an inappropriate Internet experience? If so, how was it handled and resolved? If you feel comfortable, share it with the group. It might prove beneficial.

    _____

    _____

3. How many of the following do you have in your home? Indicate who has them and where the are located.

    Computers—desktop   ___ Located _____

    Computers—laptop   ___ Located _____

    Cell phones   ___ Located _____

    Blackberries   ___ Located _____

4. Do you consider yourself to be computer savvy enough to navigate the Internet, email and related programs? Regardless of the answer, discuss why this is critically important, along with any recent personal experiences you've encountered, or information you've read or heard.

    _____

    _____

5. Why do you think kids are attracted to questionable Internet sites and online relationships even when they "know better" and are aware of a certain amount of risk involved? Why do you think they fall prey to it? Make some notes and discuss.

    _____

    _____

6. Why do you think some kids—like David in 1 Samuel 17—are able to face the "giant" head-on and consider nothing but complete victory as an option?

    _____

    _____

7. After David had slain Goliath, do you remember what Saul wanted to know about David? He asked Abner, "Who is that boy's father?" Abner said he didn't know. Saul said, "Well, go find out!" In verse 58, Saul said to David himself, "Tell me about your father, my boy."

Why did he want to know about David's father? Make some notes and discuss with the group the significance of this "father" thing. What does this say to us today about the role of the father and mother in raising responsible, courageous kids who are willing to face off the giants of our culture?

_____

_____

application

lifescene

Jared's girl friend Tamara invites him to come by her house after school one day for an hour or so. He knows his mom and Dad like Tamara, so he thinks that today would probably be OK. The first thing Tamara does is check her email and start instant messaging some of her friends, many of whom Jared doesn't know. Not only does he find out that they are from all over the country, but today one of them is recommending to Tamara some "hot" web sites she ought to check out. So she checks on a couple of them—with Jared looking on. Jared is aware of what's out there on the web, but he can't believe Tamara would open these sites, save a couple of them as "favorites," and then comment nonchalantly, "This is nothing, man. I've seen better than these!"

Later that day after Jared's mom, Elizabeth, gets home from work, she asks him how Tamara is doing, does he see her at school much, etc. She says, "The only time I ever see her is at church." Elizabeth notices that Jared's response is disturbingly brief and vague. Later that evening, she knocks on Jared's door and asks if she can come in for a moment. He says, "Sure, come on in." She goes in and comments on a couple of new photos on his bulletin board, asks about the CD that's playing, and thanks him for cleaning off the dinner table for her. Jared asks, "Is dad home yet?" Elizabeth answers, "Not yet. He said he'd be a little late tonight. Can I help you with anything?" "No," Jared says, "but when he gets home, I think I need to share something with you."

How do you think the conversation went when Dad got home? Why do you think a conversation like this is possible in the first place? Make a few notes and share your observations as to what is going on here.

_____

_____

_____

_____

prayer

Dear Father, how rewarding it would be one day for people to get to know my children, observe their character and courage, then ask about their father and mother—as if we had a lot to do with how they turned out. What a compliment that would be. I do know this for sure: we've tried to do our best, and these kids knew that they had your mighty strength inside them. I thank you that they finally learned that they would not have to fight their battles alone. They would always have you leading them and a mom and dad praying for them.

I pray, Lord, that one day when they leave home for good, they will be able to look us in the eye and say confidently, "Thanks, mom and dad, for a great life! You've packed a lot of valuable stuff in us, and now we're ready to live the way you taught us. We love you. Let's talk often!"

This is my prayer in Jesus' name, Amen.

— It's never too late to become a better parent. —

notes

notes

notes